Talking to
the Dead

Talking to
the Dead

Gordon Hodgeon

Smokestack Books
1 Lake Terrace, Grewelthorpe, Ripon HG4 3BU
e-mail: info@smokestack-books.co.uk
www.smokestack-books.co.uk

ISBN 978-0-9931490-0-9

Smokestack Books is represented
by Inpress Ltd

For John Cassidy, Sandy Cunningham, David Craig, Andy Croft, Cynthia Fuller and Richard Kell, all fine poets, talented teachers and good friends. With thanks to David Watson for agreeing to the use of a detail from his self-portrait, 'Mr. W'. Thanks also to my gang of carers, without whom many of these poems would not have been written. I have sorely tried their patience and sometimes they have tried mine. I am very grateful for all their help.

Contents

I Walked Out This Morning   9
Talking to the Dead   10
Thunderflies   11
Totentanz   12
I, Said the Fly   14
George   15
Late Lament   17
Parental   20
Solstice   21
Wed   22
Cradle Song   24
Plot   25
A Paltry Thing   26
Boris   28
After Your Visit   30
Garden Pond   32
Psalm   33
'*Mr W*'   34
Physician   35
The Words Man   37
The Good Eye   39
An die Musik   41
Wild Westerly   43
Stumm   45
Enough   46
January Twilight   47

I Walked Out This Morning

I walked out this morning
from the jigsaw jumble of
dreams and memories
and found a man in my bed
with a fly on his nose.
Only his weeping eyes could move.
I asked if I could help him
but could not understand his reply.
Oh dearie me, oh dearie him.
So I turned away to go and saw
him in the mirror standing
about to leave the room, and me
supine in the bed with a fly on my nose
and only my weeping eyes could move.

Talking to the Dead

I am talking to the dead,
who are sullen, not responding.
I try their silent language, fail
over and over. Who can teach me,
guide me through their dark palaces,
their ungrowing fields? Sometimes
one seems to speak to me, but there is
no air to carry the utterance. Faces
are blank zeros, sighs, unfathomable.
This might be a welcome, a warning.
Should I tell them what it is
I need to know or turn my back on them,
talk to the living while I can? These
seem just as incommunicado,
standing off, not wasting breath.
The sunlit living, they witness how I slide,
though they will follow me down.
I must talk with the inarticulate dead
again, learn to be one with them,
wear the common habit, nameless, and innumerable.

Thunderflies

The garden is aswarm,
minute black flies.
At once they are on me,
in my ear, on my arm.
A tickling torment.
My carer has to remove each one,
'what are they called?'

Suddenly I remember: 'Thunderflies.'
Am working with John Peake
on Tommy's farm those teenage summers,
following the reaping machine,
it throws out bundles tied with loose string.
Stooking up, one from each side,
pushing the heads of the sheaves together.
Two times four, making a tent
for the air to blow through, dry the crop.
One day no air, but thunderflies.
We looked for the darkest cloud,
a flicker of lightning, anything to drown
them, get us under the hedge.
But no thunder. Just brooding stillness,
the flies in our eyes and hair.

Back home I wash in the sink,
pull dead flies from each eye-corner,
comb a mess of them
from sun-bleached hair.

No thunder in this quiet garden,
just the flies. Time to get out of the sun,
creak up the wheelchair ramp.
Those days are lost,
most of their people dead.
Inside, free of those harbingers,
wait for the god to strike.

Totentanz

Never a star shining
down in the cold of earth.
There they are scattered,
flesh-flakes in the soil's stir,
the worm-whirls,
do they still dance it,
that thick dark winter?

Do yellowing bones still clutch
traces of DNA like an old tune
round and round in the head?
Do these spiral up in me?
If so, my connection's made
with register and census glimpses,
a few papers, family Bible,
some of their heart in there.
Infants who waltzed away
before they knew their names.

But this is not the book of the dead,
no gold leaf, no spices, no precious stones,
no feasting. Their after-life
a deep ditch, not Dante's,
paupers' graves in a crowded churchyard
in the slums they were born to.
I can only dig so far: field labourers,
mill hands, servants, colliers.
Down below that they fade
into no names, invisibility
of toil, of famine, of poverty.
They were serfs, peasants, wage slaves.

Who owned the land they lie in?
Those who made the chronicles,
history books, T.V. documentaries?
Barons, queens, factory owners, all the rest,
these in their tombs and sepulchres
with the same orchestra,
the same Okey-Cokey.

My plan is to join with
the anonymous dead,
forgotten soon enough,
no memorial stones,
I've seen too many.
I will hold hands with death
and all of you, my folk,
in the glorious dance of the earth.
Nothing but earth.

I, Said the Fly

All this last summer
you have suffered us
and wished us gone
from house and garden,
unable to lift a finger.
Bodies, you ought to know,
are painful. Now I am here
circling above your bed.
Hundreds of cells
in a convex curve: you exactly.

Aerial photography prepares the raid.
There is the white plain of your linen.
There is the outcrop of your head,
where I explore and satisfy
my curiosity. With my kith and kin,
all one, all angels, sculptors in flesh
remove the tyranny of pain,
discovering the blank ideal,
the anatomy of bone.
This is our daily bread,
our artistry and sustenance.

Now I taste your sweaty pores,
harvest the flakes of skin
among your head's sparse hairs.
I feel you thinking how the days diminish,
the rusting leaves spell autumn,
the end of our dominion.

Your relief will come with brief-sunned
winter hours in a shortening life.
We shall return, always,
the world requires us.
We shall assist you, save you,
we shall see you through.

George

for my paternal grandfather

You never reached your seventy-third birthday,
I am struggling to reach mine, so let's
get a few things straight. Through all my adult life
you've been a pain, kept slipping out
the shades, sliding your name into my affairs.
I have been George on conference lists and sticky labels,
on business letters, on hotel bills, once even on a poem.

Sometimes, so weary, I went with the flow,
so folk could go to the grave
thinking I bear your name. No chance of that.
Your only son, our father, wanted it grander,
landed me with that general's name,
my brother with Lord Clive's.
Not sure why. Dad read the *News Chronicle*.

But last Tuesday the ultimate put-down.
I was in hospital and gave my name and d.o.b.
to about fifteen nurses and my carer answered
the same questions to half a dozen doctors.
Then I got moved to my place for the night.
In comes a new nurse, greets me warmly:
'Hello George, I am Amanda, I'll be looking after you
tonight.' How do you manage it?
Have you nothing better to spend your time on?

Given the state I'm in, quite soon
we might meet up. I warn you now,
just one more trick, I'll alter every entry
in the eternal register, make sure that
all the angels and devils call you my name,
Gordon, your deserved reward.

But I'll still love you, Grandad,
love how you have walked with me
all the way, more than sixty years
from Leigh Market to just now
when I stopped walking, stopped
being able to carry your basket.

You fed the children from that grid of streets
when their dads were on strike or had no work;
you lent money, thinking it would not come back,
it didn't. You ran the Sunday School, you
made a gift to me of well-thumbed books,
Sir Walter Scott, Dickens, George Eliot.
You let me learn your sense of serious fun.
How you tormented the old ladies
reading their teacups, winking at me.

I am just as bad, laugh at my own jokes.
I never was as good at giving, never
as well-behaved, never as upright.
I should have been your namesake,
and now I see why you've been nudging,
dropping hints, not about names at all.
I let you down, still you raise me up,
George, Gordon, share this bittersweet,
this lifelong lovefeast cup.

Late Lament

i.m. Fred Hodgeon and for Julia, Libby and Ferne Sadler

Dear father, oh my father, forty years after
our last baby in the womb and your death,
I want to make you a deal, an offer
you can't refuse, while I still drag breath.
She never knew you and now she is forty,
has three daughters who delight me.

What did I ever know about you?
I saw everything with the lurid
absolutes of adolescence. Little that was true
I guess, complexities that I unmade
in my unforgiving head. You offered no defence
against tirades I know now to be nonsense.

There was your weekly flutter on the Pools.
You sat by the wireless Saturday tea time
checking the results, a win, a draw, a loss
while I played silently my little game,
predicting from the radio voice the score.
Your winnings fifteen quid over some thirty years.

Your other sin in my eyes was your smoking
which I hated and told you so too often.
I saw our money rising up in clouds, choking
mostly you. My teenage years, unsoftened
righteousness found you ridiculous.
Perhaps you were, perhaps both of us.

Your buried life I can't uncover,
and you kept quiet, not worth mention
when in my company, your clever scholar.
I guess you thought I'd give you no attention.
Probably you were right. But now I want
to hear your voice, your version, it's too late, I can't.

Instead I'll set down good things that you did,
despite your boredom, boring work and boring life.
You took me to the rugby, Kirkhall Lane and waited
after the match while I collected autographs.
Once even Bolton for a soccer game with Blackpool
with Stanley Matthews as the star, his legendary dribble.

Better than what oozes down my stubbled chin,
another charming feature of my age and state,
as I am older now than you have ever been
and dying much more slowly. Some would call this fate,
but it's a bugger anyway. I'll keep the final verses
for your heroics. Much better praise than curses.

Not a leader, then. Amen. But hero all the same.
When you saw that car swerve, head for you
and little brother, Clive, you pushed him
sideways, took the crash head on. It threw
you and the iron railings down to the street below.
That push saved his life and lost your leg. So our hero.

Here it's a rain-soaked day, one more instalment
of earth's gentle lamentation for all that lives and dies.
So all this talk is sunk, this late intent
darkens the garden plot where I see out my years.
I would seek forgiveness if I thought you could
respond from your damp grave, you can't, that's understood.

So I will sing for you, keen in my shattered glass of voice
for what won't change, then turn to these new lives
still to be written and tune to their music. I will rejoice
in all their possibilities, pray what the future gives
(I won't observe, but hope for nonetheless)
will let these three find love and loving kindness.

What you passed to me I hope to pass to my child
and to her offspring, it is love and aspiration.
Too late for grieving over our past lives, let's build
imagined futures for those who follow, our ration
of days reaching to what's beyond us.
For you from me these words and this last kiss.

Parental

When both of us are dead, you'll know
how bare your heads are to the sky,
and of those things we never told
well, any one of you might say,
if I had asked them this or that,
but too late now, the scent's gone cold.

As for your young misdeeds confessed
years afterwards, mischievousness
we never caught you at,
never thought you so bold,
well, let it go with breath
or if there's more to tell,
lay it, with us, to rest.

Solstice

It is midsummer, the evening overcast,
grey as chapels, grey as sorrow.
All the house is children's laughter,
their footsteps rattling the corridor.
From here we all go down
to the darkest day, so slow.
It is hard to imagine these children older,
dropping with the once-green, autumnal.
They are happy, unfurling, the new leaves.
I don't know what they make of me,
what they will remember or forget.
Let me enjoy them as they are
when they come to see me, the kisses
bestowed on arrival, at bedtime,
at departure. Too sick to offer
much in return, I fill with gratitude.
I watch the wood, its full-grown trees
dancing the seasons.

Wed

for Julia

Looking back, it's what we mostly do
as life draws near its close
and what I see, though slightly out of focus,
is now we have us to ourselves
more than we ever had those lengthy days
we crammed with too much work, with lovely children.

I wish we had found more time together
but then my sceptic self says best to wait
and watch conclusions leap to their various deaths.

Well I can see the point, but on the whole
will rest on what we have, I think it's love
 with all its bumps and bruises, scars
and stretch marks. We don't crave
anything different, that serves no purpose.

So no last rites, no alterations to our wills,
no codicils, no phoney looking forward
to what will be beyond us. Leave all of that
to grandchildren together with old furniture,
a few odd pictures, books, that sort of thing.

We should let things as things lie,
asleep as we are much the time.
Like all antiques we sit in silence
awaiting judgement, valuation.
Already we have lost rights
as the elderly do. Our bodies
and our minds, our very selves
commodified in medicine, in care.

What's next? We'll never know or
hardly. When it arrives, we will not be
prepared. *Die Soldaten kommen,*
die Soldaten kommen. No, not Germans,
three words drumming in my head,
an army of little deaths. Whoever,
they can take us and let the young ones go.
No beheadings, no amputations,
just the tidying up, two remnants
back to the shoddy mill. A long time newly wed,
now maybe widow and widower.

Or maybe not. Life is never so disciplined,
in stories awkward bits are shovelled
into silence through arbitrary devices
leaving life alone, let out like us
for rough grazing. We will muddle through
weeds, long grasses, nettles, our common pasture.
And share our laughter.
The slaughterhouse is always open.

Cradle Song

for Ferne, born November 2013

earth be your cradle
earth be my bed
sky be your morning light
sky my old head
sea be your appetite
sea my salt tears
days be your life to come
days my last years

let us be joined for all
the days we share
in our familial line
who went before
who still may come

and when you are grown
and I am gone
earth be your living room
earth my last house

one earth one sky one sea
our only place
one home

Plot

for Julia

So we've decided,
two daughters and one husband.
You said a cardboard coffin
buried deep in Eden.
Not sure about the box, but the plot's assured.
I'll go along with you on that.
You would approve the place,
that quiet churchyard where we walked
and often touched the Celtic cross
worn and wormed by rain.
We loved that yard and its plain church,
plain beauty as its valley, as its villages
are beautiful. We were fortunate,
until your Parkinson's, my spinal cord's
collapse brought an end.

If asked about a tombstone, I'd reply
I'm not sure but if we are to have one,
I'd choose a slab of local sandstone
likely from Lazonby, the quarries.
Few words, our names, dates, where we hailed from.
Then leave it to weather, the cling of moss,
while underground our bones might whisper
what we'd made together all those years.

No one is listening. Only faint hymns,
each autumn's brittle leaves skittering across.

A Paltry Thing

An old man now and sick,
I understand at last my dear
why sick old men retreat into
what's past and let what's passing
dive into what is still to come,
which they will never see.
It is not fear or jealousy
that drives us back
into our shrinking brains
but recognition of
where our lives are lived,
that present perfect.

I say that with some certainty,
then find my mind sticking
on the now, refusing to let go
its grip on the immediate
which roots disturbance
into what I'd thought
protected in my memory.
I tell you this who shared so much
and therefore share it still.

I never saw me following
Yeats, sailing to Byzantium
or perching on a golden bough
to sing prophetically.
But miles away in Soma
I am all ears to grief and anger
for bodies dragged into light
or lost in dark, to the damp
which stopped their breath.

That hit me hard. I had forgotten
the coalfields of my youth
and long before me when
ancestors bent to this work,
the darkness dangerous,
the air foul. Now I recall
a line of those disasters
that punctuated miners' lives with death,
left families destitute, no son, no father
to win their bread. Remains
are monuments in local cemeteries
the owners paid for, goodness of heart,
never their fault. The coal burned out
in factories, in engines, in our fireplace.
I never gave it thought. I went straight past
the morning shift as they walked home,
their dirty faces. None of them came to chapel.

I will reseal my old man's brain,
enjoy our sweet remembrances until
breaking news forces its entry. I wonder if
your mind will not keep quiet or be content
with what you have in store. I think it won't,
I think you are still open to this world
and all its sorrows, also to me,
one of its lesser pains,
an old man and a sick one
who for a while grieves over
those Turkish colliers, their families,
ponders how little changes in our lives,
the loves, the losses, hopes of song,
hymns of despair. While our music lasts.

Boris

i.m. Percy Stott

Sons of Lancashire, mid-fifties, Leigh Grammar,
Brightest and best...
we were not. Tests we were good at,
Eleven plus, then four years on
heads down for O Levels, eight or so.
But English was our pastime, we could
read and write, thought literature a joke.
Took monstrous delight in torment.
No mercy for the weak, that was you.
We sniffed you out. All was war, unfair.

Nicknames cling to teachers like stickybobs.
Mine was Greenmould, it was my suit, it was
the only suit I had, could afford. You were Boris,
you looked like Karloff in the horror films.

Your pebbled glasses, your bent back,
wild and thinning hair, all made you our target.
I watched from the back, while stars of this bloodsport
led the fray with each his special trick,
the aim a stake in the heart.

Now I lie here sixty years on and wonder what
the two of us still share apart from death,
you first, me in slow pursuit.
I don't believe we'll meet again,
but if I see your Austin 7 hugging
the middle of St Helens Road,
that primrose path, I'll hide,
then catch the bus. Once was enough.

The head taught us *Julius Caesar* drily,
I was the only one to scrape a pass.
How you survived traffic and us
I will never guess. Sorry is no excuse.
The Shakespeare, dusty as bones must be,
nearest we got to drama, except your lessons.
Mid-fifties, sons of Lancashire, Leigh Grammar.

After Your Visit

for Anna

After your visit, you waved as you passed
across the window, and I thought over
what we did not say, did not dare say,
each of us treading the edge.
I stayed looking out, watched
the last tatter of daylight shrink and die.
The dark is everywhere, reminds us.

My room's reflected on the glass.
The bookcase behind me, the lamp
in the corner, the lit corridor, my daughter
moving up and down in there
about her business, home from school,
preparing the meal, checking
the day's messages, the mail.

But I'm not there, am gone with the sun,
paled to invisible, my place is in
the company of dark shades, curtains
that frame the dusky room.
My absence fills my eyes,
erases lump of body
in this wheelchair, only the blanket left.

Sleight of the magician's palm
prefiguring that long shadow,
which leaves those books, that lamp,
even this wheelchair solid as flesh.
If anyone looks out, meets reflective self,
I'll have gone to join the dark,
not found for all their searching.

This will come, it's little wonder
we did not speak of its coming,
are come too close to it to mention.
For now we are agreed, you will send
the first email, give me an update,
I will wait impatient for summer.
Already the blossom trees are waking,
the narcissi you brought me
in full flower on the windowsill.

Garden Pond

The little pond is thick with duck weed,
frog spawn. A tight fit, I hug the murky bottom,
peer up at the obscured glass.
Someone appears, the breeze
shivers the surface, we both tremble
then become still. The trees are opening
their first flags around me and say
welcome to you. I think you are
the high clouds, the haze of sunlight.
What do you spy? Torn fragments
of a crazed plane drowning? Troops
massed on the border? All I see from here
is beyond me, the mazy weed,
the small spawn thickening, preparing
their next stage, they know nothing.
Will you come to this earth, water?
Will you observe my dead weight,
my mouthings? Not even a raised hand
summons you, but spring is about us
urgent for something we might have given.
Me in my little pond, me looking for myself
down here. It is without malice
I let you go, see to my own end,
the year's giving, taking.

Psalm

Up top this sightless moor I cry to you
from the deep self I'm drowned in.
So far away I have forgot
our bodies in the blizzard of years.

Who we were then. I am changed
ready for death when it comes.
Who you are now I do not know
alive or departed with the loss.

Our loving we thought all our lives
gone in some storm some silent morning
where are bog and stone
ogre of fell wind whisper of snowfall.

Where are you which mountain crest
which valley chiselled into rock
which plain with its despairing cities
its unknown gods its abandoned books?

Or you travel in search of some lost self
not of me I am not to be found.
I am lost in the moor's white bed
its blankness its frozen sea.

'Mr. W.'

for David Watson

Lying in bed
when my eyes are not
dribbling tears,
I observe you carefully
where you sit.
Light fades, you are alone.
Head bent to the paper,
hat obscuring your face,
you don't look up. The café
is empty, the light is fading,
you sit there, waiting
for something, somebody,
some reason to leave
the place, the table, the cups,
the drying dregs.

You will go alone
into the street's dark
remembering days,
their shades, their dim hours,
their glistening colours.
I lie here watching
my own loneliness
until lights out,
each in our separate night.
See you at sunrise,
the short day's remembrance.

Physician

Fifteen days away, now I am back
from that den of healing and see:
that thieving autumn has sneaked
into the empty garden, snatched
late blossoms, left its calling card
colouring the avenue of trees,
September sun, first warning of winter.

It was a dream with no escape,
I cried nurse nurse but they swept by.
Devils only answer their proper names,
I try from my poor stock, Belial,
Moloch, Beelzebub, Meph…
But they are past already, easy
does it. Or they are angels,
remote, indifferent. This is
no garden, no Eden, no
bower of bliss. They have
their uniform, we all have
our uniform, our grades.

We poor patients lie
or sit or wander, all
in our surgical gowns,
bare arsed, our life incurable.
I stare into the blanked-off
squares of ceiling heaven, a prisoner
aching for home, for death in its own good time,
some human requiem.

But no, the smiling crimsoned doctors
shake wise young heads, I must abide
their bloods, their protocols, must find delightful
the symphony of insane sirens.

Those fifteen days and nights had seemed
eternity, but here I am, the remnant
of a dream, in this ageing garden.
I welcome this late autumn, this approach
of winter. I will see them out or they
will bury me. I shall look forward
to the next spring, hope to admire first flowers.
But keep me safe from those cure-alls,
from their blessed rituals. It is too late
for this well meant and monstering regime.
You will find me squat amongst
our motley perennials, waiting on my last day.
Let me lie there, one with our local earth,
let me root in, lose my name,
all manacled identities.

The Words Man

Another month and two more old friends gone,
so two more empty places in my head
that won't be filled in any later season,
if any comes before I join the dead.

My brain is ageing, shrinks and gapes,
it loses systems, names, so many words
that won't leap to my clumsied lips
as they once did like young cats after birds.

This way the hole behind the eyes
gets more profound, a dizzying drop
into a last and lingering demise,
the end of all I am, have been. Full stop.

So many words, they made my voice,
but here I count the last of them,
the final drips of my rejoicing
from broken gutters of the brain.

A plenitude of rain, they filled
my seventy years with blessing,
made my soil rich and fertile,
the voice I thought unceasing.

They grew my life, from the familial
first stumblings to what I understood
was me, student, scholar,
reader, teacher, reader, poet,

made me spill volumes from my store of words
in pulpit, classroom, on the stage,
in love, in poetry. But now the clouds
have emptied, emptied most of Hodge.

The final croaks drip like a dodgy tap:
the washer is at last worn out,
syllables drown in spouts of sputum,
sputtering, secretions.

The words man. So they said,
but now, would not take the chance.
My words gone sullen, lumps of lead
misshapen gobbets of utterance.

Their ghosts stay quiet in my skull,
I'll work them secretly, bequeath
these death's head poems, rush them all
out to the deaf world, in one last breath.

The Good Eye

The good eye
acid, ice needles.
Squeeze it shut.
A tear easy
skis down the razored cheek
into the stubbly trees.

I shall soon cease
to keep this
living, this
barely evident
hard to identify
sign of a life
almost lived.

All my additions
have a time, a season.
So the stomach peg
has a life of four months,
the urine catheter lasts
four weeks in a lucky month,
sometimes and sudden it blocks
and where is the D.N. when you
need her? I could continue with
the trachi, the stoma, everything
the modern combi boiler
requires, plus annual maintenance.

Perhaps the time
to die, I can't say.
When we arrive,
realise the place, stumble
into a new grave.
The wormy soil heap by
and bought for shovels.
In we go, down we go a little way.

Everything goes down, down the hill
where the trees receive us, welcome
the final scores, the stubs of saints,
fag ends, bones of chickens, children,
what is left of you, her, him and me,
all that falls easy as palls burn,
easy as tears slither into the thorns,
freeze on the bloodied snow.

An die Musik

for Pat

I play his songs on this sad stereo,
the light and dark I find it hard to bear
as mind alone makes its Schubertiade.
Relentless years gone by since we
made pilgrimage to the real thing,
music in the clear air.

Now we are so much older,
bodies wearing out, our spirits
winter weary with the journey,
each of us seeking resolution.
For me more poems, scratches at the itch
of my decay. For you, I'm told, serenity
which calms your troubled seas. I'm glad
and hope I get a portion soon, I need it.

The sum of all our days? Perhaps not much
if we compare with his so short,
so rudely shortened life, in which
 he wandered through the groves
of music's hopes and deep despairs.
Our loving friendships walked there too
accompanied by his and others' songs.

Now Billie sings her mortal blues
and on the unread shelves the metaphysical
George Herbert sits in contemplation.
Yes we know, dear parson poet, music shows
we have our closes, all must die.

But while we live the small remainder
let's anchor in our mutual joys and griefs
and what transforms these into music
played long before and sung long after
we are returned to stardust, brief notes
in earthsong's cycle, dying, undying.

Wild Westerly

Your Atlantic-laden, shrouded skies
make the chimney groan
behind my poetry books
and at our blasted backs
that winged chariot hurtles
from the deep wreck-throated
cable-stranded sea, from the hurl
of air, of sucked-up wet.

What do you sing to me
stumbling like love from those high fells
down nearby Tees, down far off Humber?

Nothing to comfort in your mind,
you shriek of what's to come of me
as if I care, as if it matters when we all
come down to little drops of water,
shreds of flesh, ashes of bone.

I have a poet's answer to this storm
for all assembled here,
these silent legislators.
I can't read their verses now
but know their truth.
Blake, Brecht, Marlowe, Donne, Marvell,
Coleridge, Lawrence, Neruda, Keats *et al.*
Yes, we understand that you're preoccupied
with worms and what they'll try, it's natural.
You sense our brevity, the frittering of our breath,
we gutter out before we've scarce begun.
So what I'd bellow at you if I could
would go like this; we wonder, love, cry freedom, rage.
The living talk to the living in singing words,
which outlive their makers.

If you touch us, yes we will bleed.
You know I can't. But I implore you,
open any page while you have breath.
What you discover, life. Read it, devour.

Stumm

for Brian W

Stumm
is what I have become
is who I am
dumbfounded in my brain.

The din of its foundry
resounds and finds
there's no way out of
the confines of my skull.

No sound of rationality,
only the gurgling
of throaty sewers.

Otherwise stumm stumm stumm
is who I am, is what I have become.

I beat this muffled drum,
no-one has yet come to hear
my brain's impatient thrum.

Do not, oh do not blame them,
we would do the same.

That sort of said, my dear,
this dull December day
we have a little left to say.

Enough

Him and me, the two of us
on the brink, on the double white lines.
Not a pretty sight, me stuffed in the wheelchair,
him with his empty sockets, their bloody eyes
two hard boiled eggs squelched in the briny grass
into tarmacadam. No wonder the TV moguls said no
when we offered them a head-to-head. They said,
'not likely, imagine such awful visuals,
and you with your mouth agape, your dropped jaw,
saying nothing. And him just repeating his lines,
nothing we haven't heard before.' Fair point,
shall we jump? Shall we cross? In either case
he will have to push. The birds peck our bare heads,
the cars nudge our toes. Is it a sheer drop? Is there a gap?
Horns blare, birds screech, we will make a mad dash,
rush for the exit, for the free air. Wait for the crash.
Collateral, some startled sunbathers, a six-car shunt.
We have no need of fiends, other fantasticals, their horns,
their many noses, their loony eyes. Or angels.
We'll cling here on the rim to human care, to human love
until our weary flesh cries out, enough, enough.

January Twilight

for Mike

Sun wants off
quitting this grey, raggedy,
old overcoat, the garden.
Too cold out there for me,
shrivelled flowerbed,
brittle birds.

I retreat under my blanket,
again read Lawrence's
impassioned plea,
a new spring
bluebell-singing
primrose-shouting.

My dark night, I still see
flashes of our love
the bright colours
our meld of ancestors
field hands, weavers
foundrymen, colliers.

Even here, even now,
out in the garden
you can read helpless signs,
the firstblind shoots,
snowdrops, a miniature iris.
A new world. Always.